Contents

Any words appearing in the text in bold, **like this**, are explained in the glossary.

REGIONS OF THE WORLD

Eu

Neil Morris

Heinemann
LIBRARY

First published in Great Britain by Heinemann Library, Halley Court, Jordan Hill, Oxford OX2 8EJ, part of Harcourt Education.
Heinemann is a registered trademark of Harcourt Education Ltd.

© Harcourt Education Ltd 2008
First published in paperback in 2009
The moral right of the proprietor has been asserted.

Editorial: Andrew Farrow
Design: Steve Mead and Q2A Creative
Illustrations: International Mapping Associates, Inc
Picture Research: Melissa Allison
Production: Alison Parsons

Originated by Chroma Graphics (Overseas) Pte.
Printed and bound in China by Leo Paper Group

ISBN 978 0 431 90709 3 (hardback)
12 11 10 09 08
10 9 8 7 6 5 4 3 2 1

ISBN 978 0 431 90718 5 (paperback)
13 12 11 10 09
10 9 8 7 6 5 4 3 2 1

British Library Cataloguing in Publication Data
Morris, Neil
Regions of the World, Europe
Morris, Neil, 1946-
    Europe. - (Regions of the world)
    1. Europe - Geography - Juvenile literature
    I. Title
    914

A full catalogue record for this book is available from the British Library.

Acknowledgements
The publishers would like to thank the following for permission to reproduce photographs:

© Alamy: Mike Eveleigh **39**, © Corbis: Royalty-free **14**, Henrik Trygg **53**, dpa/Wolfgang Kumm **8**, epa/ESA **55**, epa/Vatican Pool **24**, Jonathan Andrew **13**, O. Alamany & E. Vicens **19**, Owen Franken **40**, Reuters/Arnd Wiegmann **27**, Reuters/Luke Macgregor **22**, Reuters/Vincent Kessler **28**, zefa/Klaus Hackenberg **4**; © PA Photos: AP Photo/ Fernando Bustamante **37**, AP Photo/Alvaro Barrientos **47**, AP Photo/Antonio Calanni **48**, AP Photo/Fabrizio Villa **15**, AP Photo/Francois Mori **36**, DPA **42**, **51**, © Photos.com **33**, © Photoshot/World Illustrated **45**, © Rex Features/Sipa Press **41**, © Robert Harding World Imagery: Bruno Morandi **52**, Simon Harris **10**, © Topfoto/Alinari Archives **38**, © UPPA/Photoshot **34** © UPPA/Photoshot/Itar – Tass **26**.

Cover photograph of the Guggenheim Museum, Bilbao, Spain: © FMGB Guggenheim Bilbao Museoa, Photo: Masterfile/Jeremy Maude, 2007. All rights reserved. Total or partial reproduced is prohibited.

The publishers would like to thank Daniel Block for his assistance in the preparation of this book.

Introducing Europe

Europe is one of the world's seven **continents**. It is the second smallest – only the continent of Australia is smaller. It stretches from the Arctic Ocean in the north to the Mediterranean Sea in the south. The Atlantic Ocean lies to the west of the continent. Europe's mainland is connected to Asia, and together these two continents make up an even bigger landmass, called **Eurasia**. The long range of Russia's Ural Mountains forms a natural boundary between Europe and Asia. The mountains divide the world's largest country, Russia. Russia spreads across both continents and forms Europe's most easterly region.

Europe is a continent with a great cultural history. Thousands of years ago, it was the birthplace of Western civilization. In southern Europe, the ancient Greeks and Romans set standards in government and culture that others have tried to follow throughout the world. In more recent centuries, Europeans led an **Industrial Revolution** that changed the way people live and work. In the 20th century, two World Wars (1914–18 and 1939–45) started in Europe and affected most of the globe.

← The flag of the European Union shows a star for each of the original 12 member states. These flags are flying outside the European **Parliament** in Strasbourg, France.

Powerful nations

For the past thousand years, Europe's history has been dominated by
the development of separate nations. Many of these nations became
very powerful over the centuries, and their development sometimes led
to great conflict. For example, the two World Wars of the 20th century
were the result of conflicts between nations. Towards the end of that
century, new European nations were created as the Soviet Union and
former Yugoslavia (see page 9) split up.

This political map shows the 45 independent countries of Europe. They include
part of the world's largest country, Russia, as well as its smallest, Vatican City.
All the countries and their statistics are listed on page 56.

European nations have had enormous influence around the world. A great age of exploration began in the 15th century, when Portuguese and Spanish sailors voyaged across the oceans into uncharted waters. They were soon followed by English, Dutch, and French explorers. The first expedition to sail right around the world returned home to Spain in 1522. The leading European nations established colonies in the Americas, Africa, and Southeast Asia. Their new empires brought an increase in trade and even more power to the Europeans. By the 19th century, the vast British Empire covered up to a quarter of the Earth's land and included about a quarter of the world's people.

Largest countries

Europe has a few large countries and many relatively small countries. The largest country by far is Russia, even though only a quarter of its land is to the west of the Ural Mountains, in the continent of Europe. Russia covers more than 40 percent of Europe's land, and is more than seven times bigger than the next largest European country, Ukraine. Both Russia and Ukraine were former **republics** of the Soviet Union (or the USSR, the Union of Soviet Socialist Republics). This **communist** state broke up into separate republics in 1991.

The next largest European country is France. France has been important throughout Europe's history, and still holds great influence today. The first French king was crowned in 987, and the country became a republic in 1792. The next largest countries are Spain and Sweden.

Dependencies

Five European countries – Denmark, France, Netherlands, Portugal, and the United Kingdom – have territories beyond their own borders. Many of these dependencies are in other parts of the world, but five are in Europe itself.

Dependencies of European countries

Dependency	Status	Area in sq km (sq miles)	Population	Location
Azores	Autonomous region of Portugal	2,247 (868)	243,000	Islands in the Atlantic Ocean
Channel Islands	British (UK) crown dependency	197 (76)	150,000	English Channel
Faroe Islands	Self-governing community of Denmark	1,399 (540)	47,000	Northern Atlantic Ocean
Gibraltar	British (UK) overseas territory	6 (2)	29,000	Southern tip of Spain
Isle of Man	British (UK) crown dependency	572 (221)	80,000	Irish Sea

↑ The Brandenburg Gate is in Germany's capital city, Berlin. It was closed in 1961, when the Berlin Wall was erected to divide the city. In 1989, following the demolition of the Wall, it was reopened. This photograph shows a ceremony in 2002 to celebrate the anniversary of the reunification of Germany and the renovation of the Gate.

Towards European unity

In the 1950s, many political leaders believed that the terrible events of the two World Wars had mainly come about because of uncontrolled **nationalism**. People believed that their own country and its culture were superior to all others, and this led to aggression towards other nations. The way to overcome this, many people thought, was to encourage closer cooperation between the nations of Western Europe.

The first steps in this process were taken by six countries – Belgium, France, Italy, Luxembourg, the Netherlands, and West Germany – when they agreed to take shared decisions about two major industries. They formed the European Coal and Steel Community (ECSC) in 1952. This organization was such a success that the six countries decided to work together in other areas of trade and industry. In 1957 they signed an agreement, called the Treaty of Rome, and set up the European Economic Community (EEC, often called the Common Market). This agreement led to taxes on trade between the six member states being reduced, and eventually abolished.

Soon other countries wanted to join the EEC (see the table opposite). In 1992, the member states agreed to cooperate on issues such as defence, law, and human rights. The EEC was incorporated into a wider organization called the European Union (EU). Since then more countries have joined, bringing the total number of members to 27. At least another three countries are due to join the EU by 2015 at the latest.

Expanding European Union

Joined 1957	1973	1981	1986	1995	2004	2007	Candidates 2010–15
Belgium France Italy Luxembourg Netherlands W. Germany	Denmark Ireland UK	Greece	Portugal Spain	Austria Finland Sweden	Cyprus Czech R. Estonia Hungary Latvia Lithuania Malta Poland Slovakia Slovenia	Bulgaria Romania	Croatia Macedonia Turkey

East vs. West

Also at this time, the western European countries were moving further apart from eastern Europe. After the end of World War II in 1945, the **capitalist** western countries were political allies of the United States. But the eastern European countries – including Albania, Bulgaria, Czechoslovakia, East Germany, Hungary, Poland, and Romania – became part of a communist bloc led by the Soviet Union. A so-called **Iron Curtain** divided Europe, and a **Cold War** developed between those to the East and the West of it. After many threats and dangerous periods, the Cold War finally ended in 1991, when the Soviet Union broke up into individual countries. East and West Germany were reunited, making Germany a single country again. Several eastern European countries

FORMER YUGOSLAVIA

In 1945, the Federal People's **Republic** of Yugoslavia was a communist state. It was governed independently from the Soviet Union, however, so it stayed out of the Cold War. In the early 1990s, tensions rose between different religious and ethnic groups in the various republics, or regions, of Yugoslavia, such as the Orthodox Christians in Serbia, the Catholics in Croatia, and the Muslims in Bosnia. Many people were killed as these republics fought within themselves and against each other. Croatia, Slovenia, and Macedonia declared independence in 1991, followed by Bosnia-Herzegovina. The remaining republics, Serbia and Montenegro, split to form two more independent countries in 2006.

Natural features

Europe's land can be divided into four main regions. The Northwestern Uplands run from northwest France to the Scandinavian Peninsula. This region has high plateaus, mountains, and many deep valleys. The lowlands of the Great European Plain cover much of the central part of the continent, from Russia to France. This region has good farmland and is the most populated part of the continent. The Central Uplands region, with its plateaus and forests, lies to the south of the Great Plain and includes the Meseta plateau (see page 13). The southern Alpine Mountains stretch all the way across the Alps (see page 14), and include the Pyrenees in the west and the Caucasus mountains in the east.

To the southeast, Europe is separated from Asia by a narrow strait that divides the country of Turkey. The European part of Turkey, which is much smaller than the Asian part, is made up of rolling plains. As the gateway to Asia, Turkey has an important role to play in European affairs. There is much disagreement in both Europe and Turkey about the country's bid to join the European Union.

← In Iceland hot, steaming water comes shooting up through a crack in the Earth. This is called a **geyser**, from the Icelandic word for "gusher".

This physical map shows Europe's main land regions.

Coastline

Europe's extensive coastline is nearly 61,000 kilometres (38,000 miles) long. It is irregular in shape, and forms a number of large peninsulas and offshore islands. In the north, the rocky coast of Norway is pierced with many deep, narrow sea inlets, called **fjords**. These were carved out thousands of years ago by **glaciers**, great slow-moving rivers of ice. The longest inlet, called the Sogne Fjord, stretches inland for more than 200 kilometres (nearly 130 miles).

With Sweden, Norway forms one of the continent's main peninsulas, called the Scandinavian Peninsula. The southwestern end of Europe is made up of the Iberian Peninsula (Spain and Portugal), which juts out into the Atlantic Ocean. The Atlantic coast is rugged, while the Mediterranean coast to the south is gentler, with many sandy beaches that are popular with holidaymakers (see page 52). Other major European peninsulas are the Apennine Peninsula (Italy) and the Balkans (mainland Greece, Albania, Bulgaria, and several other countries). Smaller peninsulas include Jutland (belonging to Denmark) and Brittany (a region of northern France).

MESETA PLATEAU

The Meseta **plateau** is a large highland area in the Iberian Peninsula. It covers nearly half the area of mainland Spain and some of Portugal, at an average height of 700 metres (2,300 feet). It is made up mainly of plains and hills, and is surrounded by mountain ranges, such as the Cantabrian Mountains to the north and the Sierra Nevada to the south. Several important rivers rise in the Meseta. These include the Tagus, which flows for more than 1000 kilometres (620 miles) through Spain and Portugal to the Atlantic Ocean, and the Guadalquivir. The plateau has a dry **climate**, with hot summers and cold winters. Spain's capital, Madrid, lies at its centre.

Islands

There are thousands of islands off the coast of Europe. The largest is Great Britain, which was once connected to the European mainland. The second largest is Iceland, which lies just south of the Arctic Circle. It is often called the "land of ice and fire", because here glaciers lie next to hot springs and volcanoes. Their heat comes from inside the Earth, since Iceland lies on a long volcanic ridge that stretches along the sea floor of the Atlantic Ocean. This underwater mountain range is called the Mid-Atlantic Ridge. Molten rock sometimes spurts through cracks in the ridge, in volcanic eruptions. The Azores islands are also part of the ridge. Iceland is about 1000 kilometres (620 miles) west of Norway, and the Azores are about 1300 kilometres (800 miles) west of Portugal.

There are also several major islands in the Mediterranean Sea. The largest of these are Sicily, Sardinia, and Corsica. Cyprus, although also an island in the Mediterranean and a member of the European Union, is geographically part of the continent of Asia.

A fjord is a narrow sea inlet, surrounded by mountains. This one is in Norway. Millions of years ago the mountains were even higher, but they have been worn away by the action of wind and water.

Mountain ranges

Although Europe's mountains are not as high as those on other continents, such as Asia and South America, there are several major mountain ranges. The Urals form the longest range, stretching roughly north-south for 2,400 kilometres (1,500 miles) across Russia, from near the Arctic Ocean to the Kazakhstan border (in Asia). Their highest peak, Gora Narodnaya, rises to 1,895 metres (6,217 feet). The mountain's lower slopes are covered with forests. Geologists believe that the Urals were first formed about 300 million years ago. The mountains are so rich in minerals that they contain more than a thousand different kinds, including gemstones.

The Caucasus range, to the south of the Urals, is only half as long but it has much higher peaks. The mountains stretch between the Black Sea and the Caspian Sea, along the boundary between Europe and Asia in Russia, Georgia, and Azerbaijan. Mount Elbrus (5,642 metres/18,510 feet), in south-western Russia, is the highest point in Europe.

Other mountain ranges, such as the Alps, form natural boundaries between countries. Good examples are the Pyrenees range, between France and Spain, and the Carpathian Mountains, between Ukraine and Romania.

The small community of Steinen in central Switzerland, to the north of the Swiss Alps, dates back to the 12th century.

The Alps

The Alps are the continent's best-known mountain range, stretching in an arc for 1,200 kilometres (750 miles) through seven countries. They begin in the west near the Mediterranean Sea, on the border between France and Italy. They then pass through northern Italy, Switzerland, Liechtenstein, southern Germany, and Austria, and end in Slovenia.

The highest Alpine peak is Mont Blanc (4,810 metres/15,781 feet), on the French–Italian border near the frontier with Switzerland. It has several long glaciers, including the Mer de Glace ("Sea of Ice").

Key dates in the history of Mont Blanc

1741	A group of English travellers records a visit to the Mer de Glace.
1786	French physician Michel-Gabriel Paccard and his guide Jacques Balmat are the first to climb Mont Blanc.
1808	Frenchwoman Marie Paradis becomes the first female mountaineer to reach the summit.
1909	A cog railway is opened to Mer de Glace (1,913 m/ 6,276 ft).
1924	The first ever Winter Olympic Games are held in the French resort of Chamonix.
1955	A cable car is built up to Aiguille du Midi (3,842 m/ 12,605 ft).
1965	A 11.6 km (7.2 miles) long Mont Blanc road tunnel opens, from Chamonix to Courmayeur (Italy).

MOUNT ETNA

Etna is the most famous volcano in Europe. It rises to 3,323 metres (10,902 feet), near the eastern coast of the island of Sicily (Italy). Mount Etna's first recorded eruption occurred about 700 BCE, and it has remained active ever since. The most recent series of major eruptions took place in 2002–03. The volcanic soil around the mountain is very fertile, and there are vineyards and orange groves on the foothills.

↑ Tourists are warned to stay away and local villagers are evacuated during eruptions of Mount Etna. This eruption occurred in 2002.

Europe's waterways

Throughout history, Europe's waterways have served as sources of water for drinking and for irrigating the land. In recent centuries, the waterway network was expanded with purpose-built canals, to carry more industrial transport. During the 20th century, some rivers were dammed so that their water power could be used to generate electricity.

Europe's longest river is the River Volga. It flows for 3,530 kilometres (2,194 miles) through Russia to the Caspian Sea. It rises in the Valdai Hills, northwest of Moscow, at a height of 228 metres (748 feet) above sea level. At its **delta** mouth into the Caspian Sea, the river is 28 metres (92 feet) below sea level. On its journey, the river receives water from about 200 **tributaries**, or smaller rivers and streams. It has been calculated that the total Volga system, including all its streams and canals, stretches for more than 570,000 kilometres (354,000 miles). The river's **basin** covers about two-fifths of the European part of Russia.

 Purpose-built canals have extended the Volga enormously, making it much more useful for industrial shipping. A 368-kilometre (229-mile) canal, called the Baltic–Volga Waterway, links the river with the Baltic Sea. In turn, this leads to the Arctic Ocean via the 227-kilometre (141-mile) White Sea–Baltic Canal. In addition, the 128-kilometre (80-mile) Moscow Canal connects the Volga to the Moskva River and the nation's capital. Finally, the Volga–Don Ship Canal connects with Europe's fifth largest river, the Don.

The ten longest rivers in Europe

River	Length in km (miles)	Outflow
Volga	3,530 (2,194)	Caspian Sea
Danube	2,850 (1,771)	Black Sea
Ural	2,428 (1,509)	Caspian Sea
Dnieper	2,200 (1,367)	Black Sea
Don	1,870 (1,162)	Sea of Azov
Rhine	1,320 (820)	North Sea
Elbe	1,165 (724)	North Sea
Vistula	1,069 (664)	Baltic Sea
Loire	1,020 (634)	Atlantic Ocean
Tagus	1,007 (626)	Atlantic Ocean

FROM THE BLACK FOREST TO THE BLACK SEA

Europe's second-longest river, the River Danube, rises as two small springs on the eastern slopes of hills in Germany's Black Forest. The river flows east through Germany, then on to the Black Sea. On its way it passes through or flows along the borders of another nine countries – Austria, Slovakia, Hungary, Croatia, Serbia, Bulgaria, Romania, Moldova, and Ukraine. The Danube flows into the Black Sea through three main delta channels, and since 1991 this region has been protected as a wildlife refuge. It is home to over 1,200 varieties of plants, 300 species of birds, and 45 freshwater fish species.

The 171-kilometre (106-mile) Main–Danube Canal, opened in 1991, connects the Danube with the River Main, a **tributary** of the Rhine. This enormously important waterway allows river traffic to travel all the way from the Black Sea to the North Sea.

River settlements

Most of Europe's major cities began as small settlements near rivers. Many cities, such as London (England) and Lisbon (Portugal) were founded near the mouth of a river (the Thames and the Tagus). The Hungarian capital of Budapest is unusual, because it grew as two separate settlements beside the Danube. In 1873, the towns of Buda (on the right, west bank) and Pest (on the east bank) combined to make the city of Budapest.

The River Danube flows through four capital cities – Vienna, Bratislava, Budapest, and Belgrade.

Major seas

Europe's three large seas are all connected to the Atlantic Ocean by narrow channels called **straits**. The largest is the Mediterranean (see below), which is linked to the Atlantic by the Strait of Gibraltar. The second largest is the Black Sea, joined to the Mediterranean by two straits called the Bosphorus and the Dardanelles. The Black Sea is in the southeast corner of Europe, near Asia. The southern shores of the Mediterranean form the coast of North Africa.

The Baltic Sea lies between the Scandinavian Peninsula and mainland Europe. It is connected to the North Sea (a part of the Atlantic Ocean east of the United Kingdom) by two wide straits called the Kattegat and the Skagerrak. More than 250 rivers empty into the Baltic Sea, making it much less salty than other seas.

INLAND SEA

Many early civilizations developed along the shores of the Mediterranean. They included the Minoan civilization on the island of Crete, and ancient Greece and Rome. The ancient Greeks called it the "Great Sea", and the Romans the "Inland Sea". We call it the Mediterranean, which means "in the middle of land".

The Mediterranean has an average depth of 1,485 metres (4,870 feet), but at its deepest point, to the south of Greece, it is 5,093 metres (16,709 feet) deep. Its northern coast is deeply indented and often mountainous, with many natural harbours. Twelve European countries share these shores: Spain, France, Monaco, Italy, Malta, Slovenia, Croatia, Bosnia-Herzegovina, Montenegro, Albania, Greece, and Turkey. In the past, the coast and sea were useful for transport and fishing. They still are today, but their most important modern benefit is as a tourist attraction.

Lakes

The world's largest lake is the salt-water Caspian Sea, which borders European Russia. The largest European lakes are in Russia, too. Lake Ladoga lies to the northeast of St Petersburg. Along with the second-largest lake, Onega, Lake Ladoga forms part of the canal system that links the Baltic Sea with the Arctic Ocean (see page 16).

Neighbouring Finland is a land of lakes. There are more than 50,000 of them, and the country's inland waters cover more than 10 percent of its total area. Many of Finland's rivers flow into these lakes, of which the largest is Lake Saimaa (4,377 square kilometres/1,690 square miles).

National parks

Most European countries have set up national parks, where regulations help to protect the environment. Many of the continent's lakes and waterways, as well as other **wetlands**, fall within these protected areas. Scientists and **environmentalists** hope that this system will help to preserve the **biodiversity** of individual regions, meaning the variety of their plant and animal species.

A good example is the Doñana National Park, on the Mediterranean coast of Andalusia in southern Spain. With its surrounding protected areas, this wetland park covers 1,300 square kilometres (500 square miles), including coastal sand dunes.

↑ The marshes and scrub of Doñana National Park in Spain form an important refuge for animals such as the Iberian lynx and the imperial eagle.

Climate

Compared with other continents, Europe has a generally mild **climate**. It is greatly affected by warm winds that blow in from the Atlantic Ocean. These winds are warmed by the Gulf Stream, an ocean current that carries warm water from the tropical Caribbean Sea up to the northern Atlantic Ocean. The Gulf Stream is caused by differences in water temperature and salinity (level of saltiness), and by the rotation of the Earth.

Europe's mild climate makes its cities generally warmer than others at the same latitude on other continents. This is shown by comparing cities in Europe, North America, and Asia. The chart compares Paris (France) with Montreal (Canada) and Harbin (China), both of which are slightly further south than the European city. Paris has milder winters and cooler summers. In terms of precipitation (rainfall or snow), Paris has less than Montreal but more than Harbin.

Temperatures and precipitation at one latitude

Location	Latitude	Average temperature °C (°F)	January temperature °C (°F)	July temperature °C (°F)	Precipitation mm (in)
Paris	48°52'N	12 (53.6)	3 (37.4)	20 (68)	619 (24.4)
Montreal	45°30'N	6 (42.8)	−10 (14)	21 (69.8)	946 (37.2)
Harbin	45°45'N	3 (37.4)	−18 (−0.4)	22 (71.6)	488 (19.2)

North-south divide

The chart below shows how southern Europe is much warmer and drier than northern Europe. In the north of the region winters are longer and colder than in southern Europe, and summers are shorter and cooler.

Temperatures and precipitation in northern and southern Europe

Location	Latitude	Average temperature °C (°F)	January temperature °C (°F)	July temperature °C (°F)	Precipitation mm (in)
Stockholm, Sweden	59°20'N	7 (44.6)	−3 (26.6)	18 (64.4)	554 (21.8)
Paris, France	48°52'N	12 (53.6)	3 (37.4)	20 (68)	619 (24.4)
Athens, Greece	37°59'N	18 (64.4)	10 (50)	28 (82.4)	402 (15.8)

GLOBAL WARMING

Studies by scientists show that the world is gradually heating up. This is partly because of the **greenhouse effect** caused by the polluting gases emitted by industrial processes, cars, aircraft, and other sources. One of the unusual effects of **global warming** may be to make parts of Europe colder. The reason for this is the Gulf Stream.

Increased temperatures are melting the ice in the Arctic region. The fresh water of the melted ice makes the sea less salty, which in turn makes it less dense so that it does not sink. This weakens the circulation of the Gulf Stream, which depends on cool water sinking in the north and travelling back south, where it warms again, rises and heads north. Studies show that the Gulf Stream has slowed by nearly 30 percent over the past 12 years. If this trend continues, it will have a major effect on Europe's climate, leading to colder winters and more storms and other forms of severe weather.

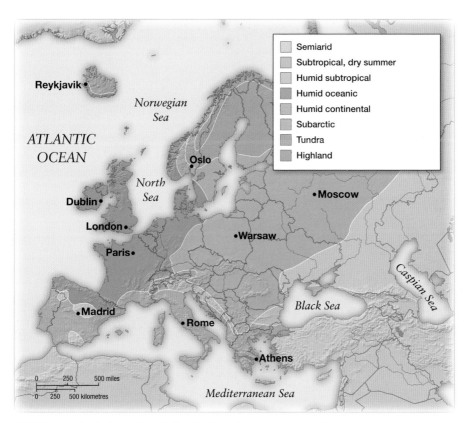

This map clearly shows the variations in climate between eastern and western Europe, as well as between the north and the south.

People

Europe has the third largest population of all the **continents**, after Asia and Africa. About 11 percent of the world's people live in the region. The European part of Russia (with more than 105 million people) is the country with the largest population, followed by Germany (82 million) and the United Kingdom (60 million).

Many of the peoples of Europe came originally from different European or Asian regions. But most have a long history in the areas they inhabit, where they have their own language, culture, and religion. Within modern nations, some ethnic groups continue to demand their own separate state and government. One example is the Basque people, who live beside the Pyrenees mountains on both sides of the border between Spain and France.

During the 20th century, there were many movements of people to and within Europe. For example, people from former British colonies in the West Indies and elsewhere moved to the United Kingdom, people from northern Africa moved to France, and people from the Balkans and Turkey moved to Germany.

← This carnival-goer is having fun at the Notting Hill Carnival in London. This three-day event has been held since 1965, and is led by Londoners with a West Indian background.

← Pope Benedict XVI stands on the balcony of St Peter's Basilica, Vatican City. A German priest called Joseph Ratzinger was elected Pope Benedict XVI in 2005, following the death of John Paul II.

Roman Catholic Church

Christianity is the dominant religion in Europe, and almost a third of the population are Roman Catholics. Catholicism has been an important force in the history of Europe and the world. During the Middle Ages, Catholic monasteries were centres of learning, and from the 16th century Catholic missionaries journeyed to Africa, Asia, and the Americas to spread their faith and European culture.

The Catholic Church dominates southern European countries such as Italy (which has more than 52 million Catholics), France, Spain, and Portugal. Catholicism is also the faith of the majority of people in Ireland (88 percent), Poland, Austria, and Hungary.

Most European countries are Christian. Muslims form the majority in Turkey (99 percent of the population) and Albania, and there are also many in Bosnia and Macedonia.

VATICAN CITY

The Roman Catholic Church is led by the pope from Vatican City, the world's smallest country, which is in Rome. With an area of just 44 hectares (109 acres), this tiny state has been an independent country since 1929. It is dominated by St Peter's Basilica, one of the largest Christian churches. The papal offices, as well as famous libraries and museums, are within the Vatican Palace. This also contains the Sistine Chapel, which is famous for its ceiling paintings by the Italian artist Michelangelo.

Protestantism

Protestants follow the tradition begun during the 16th-century religious **Reformation** in Europe. This movement was led by Martin Luther (1483–1546), a German priest who became disillusioned with the Catholic Church. Disillusion in other parts of Europe followed. By 1534, for example, the Church of England had separated from the Catholic Church and King Henry VIII had declared himself Supreme Head of the Church.

Today there are fewer than half as many Protestants as Catholics in Europe. Protestants dominate the northern countries of Denmark (with 95 percent of the population), Sweden, Norway, Finland, and Iceland. There is also a majority of Protestants in the United Kingdom, Estonia, and Latvia. Some European countries are quite evenly split: Switzerland has 42 percent Protestants and 35 percent Catholics, while in Germany the Protestant north of the country has 34 percent and the Catholic south also has 34 percent.

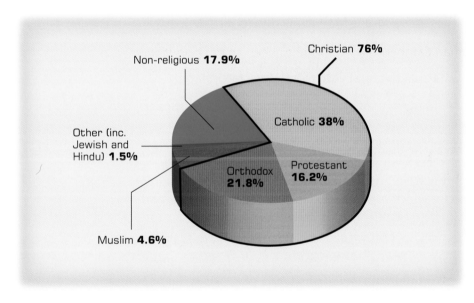

Non-religious **17.9%**

Christian **76%**

Catholic **38%**

Other (inc. Jewish and Hindu) **1.5%**

Orthodox **21.8%**

Protestant **16.2%**

Muslim **4.6%**

← This pie chart shows the different religious faiths of people in Europe.

OBERAMMERGAU

The small town of Oberammergau is in southern Germany, in the foothills of the Bavarian Alps. Every ten years the town puts on its famous Passion Play. The play tells of the crucifixion and resurrection of Jesus Christ, and includes hundreds of performers, all of whom are local residents. It was first performed in 1634 during a time of war and plague. The next Passion Play will be performed in 2010.

These see-through ballot boxes were used in the presidential election in Ukraine in 2004. It was claimed that a previous election was rigged, so there was a rerun.

Government

In Europe, governments are generally made up of members of **parliament**, or representatives, who are elected by voters in elections. Different European countries have different election regulations and voting systems. Most follow a system called **proportional representation** (PR). This gives all political parties a share of seats in parliament in proportion to their share of the total vote cast in the election.

Many people think PR is fairer than electoral systems such as "first past the post" (see below). This is because it offers candidates who represent small, minority political parties a greater chance of being elected. At the same time, it makes it less likely that one single political party will gain a majority of votes and seats in government. Because of this, PR encourages **coalition** government, which means an alliance between different parties so that they can form a government

FIRST PAST THE POST

In the United Kingdom, elections follow a traditional method called "single-member **constituency** with a simple majority". This is commonly known as "first past the post", because it is based on a candidate simply having to gain more votes than any other candidate in their **constituency** (or election area, of which there are 646 in the United Kingdom). Every voter has one vote, and each constituency elects one member of parliament (MP).

Those who defend this system say it is simpler than PR, and tends to produce a decisive result, with one political party having a clear majority of MPs. Elections for the European Parliament (see page 28), even in the United Kingdom, use proportional representation.

Integrating East and West

Since the end of communist rule and the break-up of the Soviet Union, Europe has tried to bring its eastern countries closer to the West. In one country, Germany, this brought reunification. Since the Second World War, West Germany (and now reunified Germany) has often been ruled by **coalition** governments. In 2005, Angela Merkel, leader of the conservative Christian Democratic Union party (CDU), became Germany's first female chancellor (its equivalent of a prime minister). PR elections produced a very close result, and Mrs Merkel's CDU formed a "grand coalition" with the more liberal, centre-left Social Democratic Party (SPD).

The integration of East and West has not been easy. In the former West Germany many people were unhappy at the cost of unification, which had to be paid for with higher taxes. There was a problem of growing unemployment, and many Germans began to feel that they could not support the new, enlarged country's **social welfare** budget, which looks after its most needy citizens.

← Chancellor Angela Merkel speaks in the German Bundestag (or lower house). Mrs Merkel was born in Hamburg, which was then in West Germany, but she grew up in East Germany.

European Union institutions

The European Union's Council of Ministers is made up of government ministers from the 27 member states. The Council coordinates the economic policies of the EU and approves laws proposed by the European Commission. It usually meets in Brussels. A summit meeting of member countries' heads of state or government is known as a European Council. It is chaired by the leader of the country that holds the EU presidency at that time (this changes every six months).

The European Commission is the EU's administrative and executive body. It sees that the EU's decisions are implemented, manages its budget, and proposes laws to the Council of Ministers. It is made up of a president and 26 commissioners, who serve for five years. Their job is to act for the whole of Europe, not to help the interests of their own country.

The European **Parliament** is the only part of the European Union that is directly elected by voters in member countries. There are 785 Members of the European Parliament (MEPs), who do much of their work in Brussels. The Parliament itself meets in Strasbourg, France, and has a staff of about 5,000. It watches over the activities of the other EU institutions, passes the annual EU budget, and shapes proposed new laws.

Members of the European Parliament hold up placards before voting in 2004 on whether to start membership talks with Turkey. *Evet* means 'yes' in Turkish (the same as *ja* in German and *sí* in Spanish and Italian). The 'yes' voters won the ballot.

WOMEN IN POLITICS

One of the stated aims of the European Parliament is the "promotion of genuine equality between the sexes". In many European countries, governments are trying to increase women's participation in government by encouraging more women to stand for election. Among the EU states, the percentage of women MPs ranges from a high of over 45 percent in Sweden to a low of 9 percent in Malta. The average across the EU in July 2006 was 19.5 percent.

In the European Parliament itself, 30 percent of the MEPs are women. Of the 26 commissioners, 8 (31 percent) are women. The current President of the Commission is José Manuel Barroso of Portugal. He is the 11th person to hold this office since 1958, and there has not yet been a woman president.

Temperatures and precipitation in northern and southern Europe

Country	Percentage	Country	Percentage
Sweden	45.3	Greece	13.0
Finland	37.5	France	12.2
Denmark	36.9	Slovenia	12.2
Netherlands	36.7	Hungary	10.4
Spain	36.0	Malta	9.2
average	*19.5*		

The European Court of Justice in Luxembourg is the supreme court of the European Union. It has 27 judges, chosen by agreement of the member countries. The Court judges appeals made by the Commission, the Council of Ministers, member countries, or private citizens.

Europe's role in the world

The expanded European Union has great influence in the world, and some Europeans would like to see even greater integration towards a "United States of Europe". Others would prefer to see individual countries keep their powers to govern themselves. The question of where important decisions should be taken is an enormous issue throughout Europe. Different political parties hold widely varying views. One area in which the EU has gained importance as a union is that of foreign aid. The EU is now the world's largest donor of aid, when individual donations by its member states are counted together.

Where people live

Europe's population of more than 700 million people is distributed unevenly across the continent. The region's overall average **population density** – that is, the number of people who live in one square kilometre – is about 67 (174 per square mile). Much of Europe is far less densely populated, especially the northern regions of Scandinavia. The European part of Russia (the most populous country by far), has 24 people per square kilometre (62 per square mile), and Iceland has just 3 people per square kilometre (8 per square mile).

At the other end of the scale, the tiny country of Monaco on the Mediterranean coast has more than 17,000 people per square kilometre (44,000 per square mile) and the Netherlands (which is less than half the size of Iceland) has 394 (1,020 per square mile). Of the five largest European countries, the United Kingdom has the highest population density, at 250 (648 per square mile). France has the lowest, at 109 (282 per square mile).

The map shows how the greatest population density is found near the middle of the continent. Italy has an average of 193 (500 per square mile), while Spain has less than half that number at 81 (210 per square mile).

The urban trend

As the chart opposite shows, in the past 50 years many of the world's people have been moving from the countryside (rural areas) to towns and cities (urban areas). In the near future the global urban–rural split will be 50–50, but this was already the case in Europe more than 50 years ago. The United Nations estimates that by 2015 nearly three-quarters of Europeans will live in towns and cities.

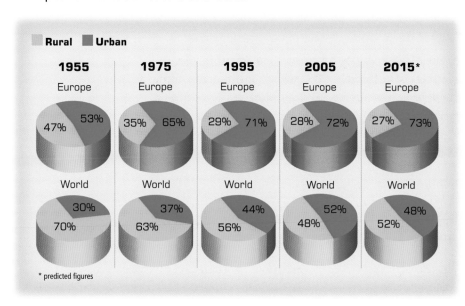

Rural Urban

| 1955 | 1975 | 1995 | 2005 | 2015* |
| Europe | Europe | Europe | Europe | Europe |

1955 Europe: 53% / 47%
1975 Europe: 65% / 35%
1995 Europe: 71% / 29%
2005 Europe: 72% / 28%
2015* Europe: 73% / 27%

World
1955 World: 30% / 70%
1975 World: 37% / 63%
1995 World: 44% / 56%
2005 World: 52% / 48%
2015* World: 48% / 52%

* predicted figures

← In 2005, 72 percent of Europeans lived in urban areas, while 28 percent lived in rural areas. The figures show how the balance has shifted towards urban living since 1955, and how this trend is predicted to continue.

Major cities

Europe has many large cities with more than a million inhabitants. In 2005, these were the largest urban areas:

Largest urban areas in Europe

City	Population in millions	City	Population in millions
Moscow, Russia	10.6	London, UK	8.5
Paris, France	9.8	Madrid, Spain	5.6
Istanbul, Turkey	9.7	St Petersburg, Russia	5.3

Many of these cities will continue to grow. In 2005, London was chosen ahead of Madrid, Moscow, and Paris (as well as New York) to host the Olympic Games in 2012. London made a strong claim for the Games by putting forward plans to regenerate a large area in the east of the city and build new sporting facilities. This is an important factor for many older European cities, where the poorer districts have become run down and need money spent on redevelopment.

Languages

About 50 different languages are spoken in Europe. Most Europeans speak a language that belongs to the Indo-European language family. This has three major branches: the Romance languages, spoken mainly in the south and including Spanish, French, and Italian; Germanic languages, spoken mainly in the north and including English and German; and Balto-Slavic languages, spoken in the east and including Russian and Polish.

In some European countries, more than one language is spoken. In Spain, for example, the official language is Castilian Spanish, which is spoken by most people. In Catalonia – the region around the city of Barcelona – many people also speak Catalan (another Romance language). In the northern region of Galicia, some people speak Galician, which is related to neighbouring Portuguese. In the Basque region they also have their own language (see below).

In the United Kingdom, other languages are spoken as well as English. In Wales there are two official languages – English and Welsh, which is a Celtic language. In Scotland and Northern Ireland, some people speak different forms of another Celtic language, called Gaelic.

NON-INDO-EUROPEAN

Some non-Indo-European languages are spoken in Europe. The Basques (see page 23) speak a language that they call Euskara. This ancient language seems to be unrelated to any other. Six dialects are spoken in the Basque country of Spain and France (the region is known to Basques as Euskadi). In eastern Europe, the Estonian, Finnish, and Hungarian languages belong to the Uralic family.

Common currency

In 2002, 12 member countries of the European Union began using the newly designed banknotes and coins of a single currency, called the **euro** (symbol €). France, Germany, Spain, Austria, Belgium, Finland, Greece, Ireland, Italy, Luxembourg, the Netherlands, and Portugal all had to give up their national currencies. Several small countries – including Slovenia, Monaco and Montenegro – also use the euro. Other EU countries will also join the euro area – often called Euroland – but Denmark, Sweden and the United Kingdom have voted not to adopt it. Although many people living in the euro countries were unsure about the new currency,

↑ Euro bank notes are the same for all the countries that use them. Euro coins have a common side and a national side, with an image representing the country that issued the coin.

they have taken to it well. Most enjoy being able to move around Europe without having to change their money to a different currency.

Moving between countries

Migration between EU countries is relatively easy, because citizens have the right to live, travel, and work in the country of their choice within the EU. However, as more migrant workers arrive in Europe, some people think there should be more restrictions. For example, in 2006 the UK government worked out that about 600,000 people had moved to the United Kingdom to work from the eight countries that joined the European Union in 2004.

There is a great debate within Europe about the more controversial question of **immigration** from outside Europe. **Asylum seekers** arrive from countries such as Afghanistan and Iraq, as refugees from war and persecution. Most countries will allow a certain number of genuine asylum seekers (rather than **economic migrants**, who are simply looking for work). In Spain, illegal (not officially welcomed) immigrants come from North African countries such as Morocco. An opinion poll in Spain found that 60 percent of Spanish people think that immigrants are responsible for an increase in the level of crime.

Culture

The arts, customs, and ways of life of Europeans are as varied and important as the many different countries and ethnic groups that make up the **continent**. European culture is based on a long tradition of success and innovation in such fields as painting and sculpture, architecture and design, dance, music, and opera, and drama and literature. This has made Europe famous for its individual artists, as well as for those involved in the popular culture of more modern times.

In the 14th and 15th centuries, a new cultural movement developed in Europe which influenced the whole world. This was the Renaissance (French for "rebirth"), whose artists were greatly influenced by the works of ancient Greece and Rome. This movement produced such great Italian painters as Leonardo da Vinci and Michelangelo, among many other artists and architects. Many of today's tourists – from Europe and other continents – visit the towns, galleries, and museums where they can see the work of these past masters.

← This catwalk model presents a dress from the Parisian fashion house of Emanuel Ungaro.

↑ The *Mona Lisa*, painted by Leonardo da Vinci in about 1503, is one of the most famous
pictures in the world. Visitors flock to the Louvre Museum, in Paris, to see the original.

Art movements

Throughout the 20th century, European artists built on past traditions
and created new directions and movements in painting and other art
forms. The first new movement of the century was Fauvism, led by French
artist Henri Matisse (1869–1954), which included a vivid, colourful style
of painting that flourished in Paris. This was followed by the Cubist style
developed by Pablo Picasso (1881–1973) and Georges Braque (1882–1963).
This reacted against earlier ideas of representation and introduced unusual
perspectives.

German Expressionism (expressing the emotional experience of the artist)
developed in two groups, in Dresden and Munich. Its leading exponents
were Ernst Ludwig Kirchner (1880–1938) and Russian-born Wassily
Kandinsky (1866–1944). The Dutch abstract movement of De Stijl ("the
style") was founded by Piet Mondrian (1872–1944). It was followed by the
amazing Surrealism of artists such as Salvador Dalí (1904–89) of Spain, Max
Ernst (1891–1976) of Germany and René Magritte (1898–1967) of Belgium.

Current European artists, are portraying their experiences in their own
individual ways. Many combine different media, such as painting,
sculpture, and moving images, to add to their expression.

Fashion capitals

London, Milan, and Paris are the fashion capitals of Europe and, with New York and Tokyo, the world. Celebrated fashion designers work here, and this is where the major fashion houses (or companies) have their headquarters. All three cities hold fashion weeks in the spring and autumn, when designers show their new collections. Buyers for major clothing stores, fashion writers, critics, and celebrities attend the shows, where famous models display the latest offerings on the catwalk.

BUILDINGS AND BRIDGES

Many European architects are at the forefront of modern design. One of the most successful and interesting is Santiago Calatrava, who was born in 1951 in Valencia, Spain. He was influenced by Le Corbusier (1887–1965), an inventive French-Swiss architect. Calatrava has designed many buildings, including opera houses, art galleries, towers, railway stations, and airport terminals. Some of his most famous works are bridges. These include three across a canal in the Netherlands that look like and are named after medieval stringed instruments – the harp, lute, and lyre.

Santiago Calatrava designed this opera house, which opened in Valencia, Spain, in 2005. The hall's four performance spaces hold 4,000 seats and form part of a complete Centre for Arts and Sciences.

La Scala in Milan, Italy, is one of the world's most famous opera houses. It has its own resident orchestra, and the fine 18th-century building has recently been renovated.

Composers and orchestras

Classical music has a long tradition in Europe. In the 18th century, two German composers, Johann Sebastian Bach (1685–1750) and George Frederick Handel (1685–1759) took Baroque music to its peak. They were followed in the classical period by the Austrian composers Franz Joseph Haydn (1732–1809) and Wolfgang Amadeus Mozart (1756–91), and by Ludwig van Beethoven (1770–1827) of Germany. All three wrote great symphonies for large orchestras.

Today, a large number of great European orchestras carry on the traditions of classical music, playing symphonies from the 18th–20th centuries, as well as modern works. They include the Vienna Philharmonic (founded in 1842), as well as the philharmonic (meaning "devoted to music") orchestras of Berlin, London, Oslo, St. Petersburg, and Warsaw.

SALZBURG FESTIVAL

More than 2,000 annual music and arts festivals are held in Europe. One of the oldest and most famous takes place in the beautiful Austrian city of Salzburg, where Mozart was born. The first music festival was held there by the Mozart Foundation in 1877, and the tradition of the summer Salzburg Festival began in 1920. It continues to this day. The festival presents performances of concerts, operas, and plays over a period of six weeks each summer. World-famous orchestras, conductors, instrumentalists, singers, and actors can all be seen at the festival.

Traditional music

Many of the different ethnic groups of Europe have developed their own traditional songs and dances down the centuries. This is often called folk music. Its various forms are still popular today. A good example is the Portuguese music called *fado* (meaning "fate"), which is generally performed by a female singer accompanied by a guitarist. The music, which is normally made up of sad songs about Portuguese life, has a long tradition in the capital city, Lisbon.

A *fado* singer entertains her audience in Lisbon, Portugal. This traditional music may have originated in the city early in the 19th century.

Popular music

Most forms of modern popular music, such as rock and pop, originally developed outside Europe, in the United States. Nevertheless, since the 1960s and the worldwide success of pop groups such as the Beatles and the Rolling Stones, there has been a strong tradition in Europe. They were followed in the 1970s by rock bands Led Zeppelin and Pink Floyd, both of which sold more than 40 million copies of their albums worldwide. Today they have been replaced by new European bands, though in 2006 the Rolling Stones were still making records and touring Europe.

Food and drink

There are different **culinary** traditions across Europe, and diets vary according to the **climate** and the availability of ingredients. However, regional varieties are less marked today, as we are used to eating food from all over the world.

Probably the most famous style of cooking is French *haute cuisine* (meaning "high-quality cooking"). French people consider cooking an art, and they hold their chefs in high regard. Whether they are eating at home or in a restaurant, the French expect high standards and use high-quality ingredients.

← Young people from all over the world go to Paris and other French cities to learn the skills of *haute cuisine* at culinary schools.

ITALIAN PIZZA

Italian cooking is very regional, and many Italians say there is no such thing as "Italian food". They prefer to talk about Tuscan or Sicilian cooking, for example. One of their world-famous dishes comes originally from the southern city of Naples – pizza. It is said that the round bread-dough dish with various toppings was popular with the poor of Naples in the 18th century. It became known in the rest of Italy after Queen Margherita of Savoy enjoyed a slice of pizza in 1889. Italian emigrants took pizza recipes with them to other European countries and especially America, making pizza one of the world's most popular foods.

Sporting traditions

Many major sports were first played in Europe, including the world's most popular sport – football, or soccer. The first proper rules for "association football" were written at Cambridge University, England in 1843, and the English Football Association was formed 20 years later. Today, 207 national associations belong to the world governing body of soccer, FIFA.

Many European countries also have their own sporting traditions. The British invented the game of cricket, which dates back to the 16th century. They took the game with them to parts of their large empire in the 18th and 19th centuries, so that today cricket is still an important sport in Australia, India, Pakistan, South Africa, West Indies, and many other Commonwealth countries. It is also played in other European countries, such as the Netherlands and Ireland.

Other traditional sports have remained more regional. Pelota, for example, is a ball game that has been played in the Basque region of northeast Spain and southwest France for centuries. It is played in different variations by hitting a ball against a wall using your hand, a racket, a wooden bat, or a basket. It is still much loved in the Basque region, and emigrants have taken the game to several South American countries.

Many millions of people around the world watched the football World Cup finals held in Germany in 2006. Italy beat France in the final.

Natural resources and economy

Europe is rich in natural resources, including coal, iron, forests, and large areas of fertile soil. The availability of coal and iron helped to bring about the **Industrial Revolution** in the 18th century, which made northern Europe the birthplace of modern industry. British and other European manufacturers were the first to use power-driven machinery, which increased levels of production and lowered costs. This development made several European nations leading centres of industry.

Today, the European Union forms the world's second-largest economy (after the United States), with Germany, United Kingdom, France, Italy, and Russia the strongest national economies in Europe. Products such as steel, textiles, and cars are still important in manufacturing, but the production of electronic equipment and other high-tech goods has grown in importance. At the same time, more than half of all workers are employed in service industries, such as banking, retail, education, and tourism. The European economy is changing in nature, but it remains strong.

← This steel is being manufactured in Germany, Europe's biggest steel producer. In 2005, Germany made nearly a quarter of the region's steel, and Europe produced a fifth of the world's steel.

Energy sources

In the 20th century, European countries relied mainly on **fossil fuels** (coal, oil, and natural gas) to provide most of their energy. Russia (including its Asian region), Poland, and Ukraine are the largest coal-producing nations and, as the table below shows, many European countries are still very dependent on coal for producing their electricity. Russia is the world's leading producer of natural gas, and many other European countries import gas from Russia, some through long pipelines. Oil from beneath the North Sea is not as plentiful as it was, and some European countries are very dependent on imported oil. But all fossil fuels are non-renewable – they cannot be replaced and will one day run out – so many countries are looking to increase their use of renewable sources.

The chart below shows Europe's top ten biggest economies (in order from top to bottom), plus Norway and Iceland for comparison. The largest energy source for each country appears in bold.

Percentage of energy sources used to produce electricity

	coal %	oil %	gas %	nuclear %	renewables %
Germany	**52.9**	0.8	9.8	27.8	8.7
UK	35.4	1.8	**37.5**	22.4	2.8
France	5.3	1.5	3.1	**78.5**	11.6
Italy	15.6	26.8	**41.4**	0.0	16.2
Russia	18.8	3.0	**44.5**	16.4	17.3
Spain	**29.5**	9.3	15.3	24.0	22.0
Turkey	22.9	6.5	**45.2**	0.0	25.3
Netherlands	28.4	3.0	**58.8**	4.2	5.7
Poland	**95.1**	1.6	1.6	0.0	1.7
Ukraine	18.3	0.5	30.9	**45.2**	5.1
Norway	0.1	0.0	0.3	0.0	**99.6**
Iceland	0.0	0.1	0.0	0.0	**99.9**

Renewable sources

Renewable sources of energy include: **hydroelectric** (or water) **power** from river dams, tidal barrages, and ocean wave devices; wind power; solar power; geothermal power from heat inside the Earth; and **biomass** power from plant and animal material, including waste.

As well as being renewable, these energy sources have the advantage that, unlike fossil fuels, they give off little or no carbon dioxide and other greenhouse gases that may be contributing to **global warming**. In Iceland, much renewable energy is from a geothermal source using heat from the Mid-Atlantic Ridge (see page 12) to make electricity and heat homes.

This hydroelectric dam is in Norway. Water power produces 98.9 percent of the country's electricity.

THE NUCLEAR DEBATE

European countries are divided on the issue of using of nuclear power as a source of energy. France is totally committed to it, Italy is completely against it, while many others see it as a useful part of their mix of energy sources. Nuclear power has advantages: it produces a huge amount of energy from a small amount of fuel (non-renewable uranium), and does not release carbon dioxide. But it has huge disadvantages too: possible accidents at nuclear power stations (such as happened at Chernobyl, Ukraine, in 1986), problems in disposing of radioactive waste, the link with nuclear weapons, and the possibility that terrorists might get hold of nuclear material.

Agriculture

Europe has large areas of fertile farmland. About half of its cropland is used to produce grain, especially wheat and barley. Other important crops are oats, rye, potatoes, and sugar beet. In the warm south, olives, citrus fruits, dates, figs, and grapes are grown, and more than three-quarters of the world's olive oil comes from this southern region. Dairy farming is important in the United Kingdom, Denmark, and the Netherlands, and cattle, pigs, sheep, and poultry are raised in most parts of the **continent**.

The size of farms varies enormously across the region, from family smallholdings to large agricultural businesses. The average size of a UK farm is 69 hectares (171 acres, more than 2.5 times smaller than the average US farm). In Germany it is 43 hectares (106 acres), while in Greece it is just 4 hectares (10 acres).

COMMON AGRICULTURAL POLICY

In 1962, the European Economic Community (EEC, now the EU) introduced the Common Agricultural Policy (CAP). This had five stated aims: to increase productivity, to ensure fair living standards for farmers, to stabilize markets, to ensure availability of food, and to provide food at reasonable prices. The CAP subsidized agricultural exports, taxed imports, and bought produce when its market price fell below a certain level. This system led to huge overproduction, with unwanted "mountains" of butter and beef, and "lakes" of milk and wine. There was heavy criticism from many people, but some European countries – especially France – believe that these farming subsidies are essential to help their rural economy. They ensure that food is safe to eat, and that there are high standards of animal welfare and environmental protection. However, critics say that the policy prevents the export of agricultural goods from the developing world into Europe, especially from African countries. They believe that the low European prices of goods are making it impossible for Third World farmers to compete, and putting them out of business. The CAP is currently in the process of reform.

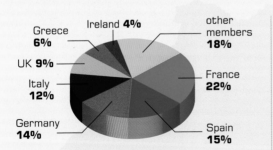

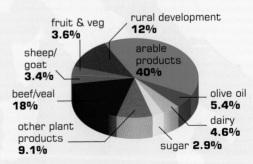

These charts show which countries received most money from the CAP in 2004, and what that money was spent on.

Fishing

Europe has a long coastline, and fishing is an important industry. During the 20th century, many countries changed from having small, local fishing fleets to large ocean trawlers. This led to over-fishing, so that stocks of staple fish, such as cod and herring, became very low in European and other waters. The top fishing countries in Europe are Russia, Norway, and Iceland, though together they take only about half the annual catch of China, the world's leading fishing nation.

Following the European Union's Common Fisheries Policy (CFP), restrictions had to be introduced and quotas (limits on the size of catches) were forced on the fishing community. The aim was to help stocks of staple fish recover. The policy was not popular with many fleets, especially smaller ones, and there have been many protests, but **environmentalists** and food specialists agree that over-fishing is a big problem. The restrictions have resulted in fewer people working in the fishing industry. In Norway, the number has fallen by 20 percent over the past ten years, and in Iceland by 14 percent.

Fishermen have blocked this port in northern Spain, to protest against rising fuel prices and dropping fish quotas.

Manufacturing industry

Manufacturing industry is very strong in western Europe. Several areas in the region are well known for heavy industry, such as steel making and engineering. The best example is the Ruhr district of Germany, which includes the industrial cities of Dortmund, Duisburg, Düsseldorf, Essen, and Wuppertal. The Ruhr (named after the River Ruhr, a **tributary** of the Rhine) produces chemicals, textiles, and especially iron and steel. In recent years, areas such as the Ruhr have had to modernize and learn to manufacture new products, such as kitchen appliances and electronic equipment. This has brought them into competition with manufacturers in the Far East.

The first motor cars were built in Europe towards the end of the 19th century. Today, European factories still produce more than a third of the world's passenger cars (see table opposite). Germany is the biggest car producer in Europe, with brands such as Volkswagen, BMW, and Mercedes. Worldwide, it is second only to Japan (9.0 million cars) in output. France is the fourth largest producer in the world, behind the United States (4.3 million) and level with China.

Italy is famous for its sports cars, including the Ferrari, which is here being made at the Maranello factory. But in 2005 Italy's car output was nearly 30 percent less than it had been in 2003.

Passenger cars produced in 2005

	Cars in millions	% of world production
Europe	17.6	38.3
EU countries	**15.8**	**34.3**
Germany	5.4	11.7
France	3.1	6.7
Spain	2.1	4.6
UK	1.6	3.4
Russia	1.1	2.3
Belgium	0.9	2.0
Italy	0.7	1.5
Czech Republic	0.6	1.3

TRANSPORT LINKS

The Ruhr district has an excellent network of roads, railways, rivers, and canals. Transport links were recognized as being important in the early days of the **Industrial Revolution**, when engineers built canals and bridges close to mines and factories. Today, it is more important for many industries to be close to transport links than to their raw materials (which may be imported). Many new industries, such as computer and other electronics firms, have set up or relocated close to ports, motorways, and large cities.

Modernization and globalization

Since the early 1990s, there have been big changes in much of eastern Europe. Old machinery has been updated or replaced, and industrial cities such as Dresden (in the former East Germany) have been modernized. In many cases, however, modern methods (such as industrial robots used to weld car parts together) have created high levels of unemployment in former industrial areas. At the same time, many European firms have become part of huge, international companies that operate globally. Goods or parts of goods may be assembled in Europe by companies whose headquarters are in New York, Seoul, or Tokyo. For example, in 1989 the Japanese car manufacturer Toyota opened a factory near Derby, in the United Kingdom. The idea was to make Japanese cars for the European market. But four years later, the company was also exporting British-made Toyota cars to Japan.

Economy and wealth

A country's economy includes its production and consumption of goods and services. The economic performance of European countries varies enormously, and national economies are not growing at an even rate across the continent. The richer industrial countries – such as Germany, United Kingdom, France, Italy, and Russia – continue to gain wealth at a faster rate than the poorer countries, such as Moldova, Montenegro, and Serbia.

Figures for **gross domestic product** (GDP) show how the economic performance of one country compares with that of others. GDP is the total value of a country's goods and services (not including any extra income from investment in other countries). The chart below shows Europe's top five and bottom five countries for GDP per person, with the EU average in the middle. The figures show that unemployment is much higher in the poorer countries. While Luxembourg comes out at nearly twice the EU average, Moldova has just one fifteenth the average. In 2001, it was estimated that 80 percent of the population of Moldova, the poorest country in Europe and not an EU member, was living in poverty. This was partly because many unemployed Moldavians have left to find work in neighbouring countries. In 2005, the European Union drew up an action plan to help Moldova develop its economy.

Gross domestic product (GDP) per person in Europe

	GDP per person in thousands of US$	% of people unemployed
Luxembourg	55.6	4.5
Norway	42.3	4.6
Ireland	41.0	4.3
Iceland	35.6	2.1
Denmark	34.6	5.7
European Union	**28.1**	**9.4**
Bosnia	6.8	45.5
Albania	4.9	14.3
Serbia	4.4	31.6
Montenegro	3.8	27.7
Moldova	1.8	8.0

QUALITY OF LIFE AND EDUCATION

The United Nations Human Development Index is a way of comparing people's standard of living and quality of life. The index takes into account each country's levels of wealth, education, literacy, life expectancy, childbirth, and other factors. In its 2005 report, the Index placed Norway first in the world for human development, Iceland second and Luxembourg fourth. Altogether there were 15 European countries in the world's top 20, including the United Kingdom, France, Italy, and Germany. (The non-European countries were Australia, Canada, United States, Japan, and New Zealand).

Standards of education are an important factor in the Index. Education provides the qualified workforce needed to improve the economy, but it is also affected by the economy, because rich countries can spend more on it. Norway and Sweden spend nearly 8 percent of their GDP on education, while Romania spends 3.5 percent.

Pollution

The industrialized countries of eastern Europe have traditionally had a lot of heavy industry, such as steel making and engineering. This has created high levels of pollution in recent decades. The European Union has introduced new environmental regulations and initiatives, to make governments look at ways to improve and protect the environment. These include limiting the emission of greenhouse gases, the conservation and improvement of water resources, and recycling projects to improve waste disposal.

This large recycling centre is in the iron and steel town of Eisenhüttenstadt in eastern Germany.

This beautiful Mediterranean bay is on the Italian island of Sardinia.

Tourism

Tourism is an extremely important industry in Europe. More than 415 million people took holidays in Europe in 2004, an increase of 5 percent on the previous year. This includes Europeans travelling to another country within the continent. Tourism is big business. Altogether it produces about 10 percent of Europe's GDP (see page 50), and 2 million tourist firms employ up to 20 million people.

France, Spain, Italy, the United Kingdom, and Germany receive the most tourists. Many of the visitors to France, Spain, and Italy take beach holidays along the Mediterranean coast. In recent years the number of visitors has been rising. This has put a strain on the environment, by increasing the amount of pollution and the use of resources such as fresh water.

SUNNY COAST

The Costa del Sol, on the southern Spanish Mediterranean coast, runs for 160 kilometres (100 miles), from east of Gibraltar to Malaga and has an average of 300 days of sunshine a year. The towns and beach resorts have been developed over the past 50 years. There are more than 30 golf courses just inland. The beaches and sporting activities attract about 8.5 million tourists each year, 31 percent of them British. More than a third of the visitors arrive by plane. In 2005, the area suffered from drought and water shortages, which threatened the tourism industry. With the predictions of global warming, many southern European tourist regions will have to put in place plans for water conservation.

Biggest tourism regions in the world

According to the European Environment Agency, the Mediterranean is the biggest tourism region in the world. The Alps have the second highest tourism intensity in Europe, with 60 million visitors a year. They are popular for winter sports such as skiing. France, Switzerland, Austria, Italy, and Germany have many famous alpine resorts.

As in the Mediterranean, the combination of more visitors and **climate** change is affecting the Alps. Some of the lower ski resorts have experienced a lack of snow in recent years, and many have installed artificial snow machines. The ski slopes have become increasingly busy, but skiing outside the recognized areas and tracks increases the danger of avalanches.

These people are enjoying cross-country skiing in Sweden. This form of skiing has become more popular in recent years.

Transport

Europe has an extensive network of roads and railways. Germany built the first European motorways (*Autobahnen* in German), in the 1930s. It still has the most motorways in western Europe (more than 11,700 kilometres/7,270 miles), ahead of France (10,100 kilometres/6,280 miles) and Spain (9,600 kilometres/5,970 miles). Including its Asian territory, Russia has 46,000 kilometres (28,600 miles) of motorways. Germany also has a high rate of private car ownership (541 cars per 1,000 people), though Liechtenstein (682), Luxembourg (629), Andorra (600), Italy (581), Iceland (563), and Portugal (558) have more. These figures compare with 765 cars per 1,000 people in the United States.

Concerns about pollution from car exhausts and the overuse of roads have led to calls for improved public transport in many European countries. Germany leads Europe with the greatest length of railway (36,600 kilometres/22,700 miles), though Russia has 85,800 kilometres (53,300 miles) including its Asian lands. In German, French, and other European cities, efforts are being made to link buses, trains, and trams into an integrated system, to encourage people to use their cars less. In London, a congestion charge, or fee, has been introduced to discourage people from driving into the city.

FRENCH HIGH-SPEED TRAIN

France has more than 31,300 kilometres (19,400 miles) of railway track. About 1,200 kilometres (750 miles) of it are suitable for use by the fast French *Train à Grande Vitesse* (TGV, or "high-speed train"), which was introduced on a service from Paris to Lyon in 1981. Since then, the service has been extended to Lille and Brussels (the capital of Belgium), and south to Marseilles. The electric TGVs travel at up to 320 kilometres per hour (200 miles per hour) on normal services, and have travelled much faster on test runs. The TGV holds the world speed record for a conventional train – 573 kilometres per hour (356 miles per hour)!

More high-speed tracks are being laid to connect France with the United Kingdom, the Netherlands, Germany, Switzerland, and Italy. In 1994, the 50-kilometre (31-mile) Channel Tunnel between France and England opened for rail traffic. Railway tracks in the United Kingdom are being upgraded so that London can be added to the high-speed rail network.

European space exploration

The European Space Agency (ESA) was founded in 1975, with a mission to "shape the development of Europe's space capability and ensure that investment in space continues to deliver benefits to the citizens of Europe". ESA is funded by 17 member states: Austria, Belgium, Denmark, Finland, France, Germany, Greece, Ireland, Italy, Luxembourg, the Netherlands, Norway, Portugal, Spain, Sweden, Switzerland, and the United Kingdom. Its headquarters are in Paris, and it launches many of its rockets from a site in French Guiana (a **dependency** of France in South America). The Agency's projects are designed to find out more about the Earth, the solar system and the universe, as well as to develop space technology and promote European industries. In 1985, ESA launched the space probe *Giotto*, which took photographs as it passed within 600 kilometres (370 miles) of Halley's Comet. In 2005, it sent an unmanned mission to Venus.

ESA's Venus Express spacecraft was launched by a Soyuz-Fregat rocket at the Baikonur Cosmodrome, in Kazakhstan, on 9th November 2005. It entered orbit around Venus in April 2006, ready to study the planet's atmosphere and surface.

Fact file

Independent countries of Europe

Name	Area in sq km (sq miles)	Population*	Capital
Albania	28,748 (11,100)	3,187,000	Tirane
Andorra	468 (181)	79,000	Andorra la Vella
Austria	83,871 (32,383)	8,221,000	Vienna
Azerbaijan (European)	14,300 (5,521)	2,582,000	Baku
Belarus	207,600 (80,155)	9,615,000	Minsk
Belgium	30,528 (11,787)	10,490,000	Brussels
Bosnia-Herzegovina	51,197 (19,767)	3,923,000	Sarajevo
Bulgaria	110,912 (42,823)	7,549,000	Sofia
Croatia	56,538 (21,829)	4,392,000	Zagreb
Czech Republic	78,866 (30,450)	10,205,000	Prague
Denmark	43,094 (16,639)	5,463,000	Copenhagen
Estonia	45,100 (17,413)	1,334,000	Tallinn
Finland	338,145 (130,559)	5,285,000	Helsinki
France	551,500 (212,935)	61,225,000	Paris
Germany	357,022 (137,847)	82,414,000	Berlin
Greece	131,957 (50,949)	11,128,000	Athens
Hungary	93,032 (35,920)	10,020,000	Budapest
Iceland	103,000 (39,769)	300,000	Reykjavik
Ireland	70,273 (27,133)	4,269,000	Dublin
Italy	301,268 (116,320)	58,818,000	Rome
Latvia	64,589 (24,938)	2,267,000	Riga

Liechtenstein	160 (62)	36,000	Vaduz
Lithuania	65,300 (25,212)	3,374,000	Vilnius
Luxembourg	2,586 (998)	469,000	Luxembourg
Macedonia	25,713 (9,928)	2,048,000	Skopje
Malta	316 (122)	409,000	Valletta
Moldova	33,800 (13,050)	3,982,000	Chisinau
Monaco	1.95 (0.75)	34,000	Monaco
Montenegro	13,812 (5,333)	629,000	Podgorica
Netherlands	41,528 (16,034)	16,513,000	Amsterdam
Norway	385,199 (148,726)	4,671,000	Oslo
Poland	312,685 (120,728)	38,077,000	Warsaw
Portugal	88,941 (34,340)	10,678,000	Lisbon
Romania	238,391 (92,043)	21,517,000	Bucharest
Russia (European area)	4,309,400 (1,663,869)	104,605,000	Moscow
San Marino	61 (24)	29,000	San Marino
Serbia	88,361 (34,116)	9,519,000	Belgrade
Slovakia	49,033 (18,932)	5,395,000	Bratislava
Slovenia	20,273 (7,827)	2,001,000	Ljubljana
Spain	505,992 (195,365)	44,687,000	Madrid
Sweden	449,964 (173,732)	9,179,000	Stockholm
Switzerland	41,284 (15,940)	7,542,000	Bern
Turkey (European area)	23,621 (9,120)	8,231,000	Ankara (in Asia)
Ukraine	603,700 (233,090)	46,060,000	Kiev
United Kingdom	242,900 (93,784)	60,590,000	London
Vatican City	0.44 (0.17)	1,000	—

*Populations are 2008 estimates, based on the latest figures from official government and United Nations sources.

Although Cyprus is a member of the European Union, geographically it is part of the continent of Asia so it is not included here.

Timeline

c. 3000 BCE	The Minoan civilization develops on the island of Crete; the start of the building of Stonehenge, a great stone circle in England.
1500–1150 BCE	The Mycenaean civilization dominates mainland Greece.
776 BCE	The first Games are held at Olympia, Greece (ancient Olympic Games).
753 BCE	The legendary date of the founding of Rome.
500–300 BCE	The ancient Greek civilization reaches its height.
490 BCE	The ancient Greeks defeat the Persians at the Battle of Marathon.
44 BCE	Julius Caesar is assassinated in Rome.
27 BCE–14 CE	The reign of the first Roman emperor, Augustus.
324 CE	The Roman emperor Constantine moves his capital to Constantinople (Byzantium).
395–1453	The period of the Byzantine (Eastern Roman) Empire.
476	The fall of the (Western) Roman Empire.
711	Muslim Moors invade Spain.
800	The Carolingian King Charlemagne is crowned Holy Roman Emperor.
874	Vikings settle in Iceland.
1054	A split occurs between the Roman Catholic Church and the Eastern Orthodox Church.
1066	The Normans conquer England.
1096–1291	The Crusades – European Christian military expeditions to Palestine.
1337–1453	The Hundred Years' War between England and France.
1347–52	The Black Death plague kills about a quarter of Europe's population.

1492	Spain is reconquered as the Moors lose Granada.
1517	Martin Luther starts the Protestant Reformation in Germany.
1618–48	The Thirty Years' War involves many European nations.
1689	The Bill of Rights establishes a constitutional monarchy in England.
1789–99	The French Revolution ends the monarchy in France.
1815	Napoleon is finally defeated by the English at the Battle of Waterloo.
1837–1901	Queen Victoria reigns over the United Kingdom of Great Britain and Ireland; she becomes Empress of India in 1876.
1914–18	World War I, in which the Allied Powers of the United Kingdom, France, Russia, Belgium, Japan, Serbia, Italy, Portugal, Romania, the United States, and Greece defeat the Central Powers of Germany, Austria-Hungary, Turkey, and Bulgaria.
1917	The Russian Revolution overthrows the monarchy and establishes a **communist** state.
1922–91	The period of the Soviet Union, a state made up of 15 communist **republics** including Russia.
1933	Adolf Hitler becomes chancellor of Germany.
1939–45	World War II, in which the Allied Powers of the United Kingdom, Commonwealth countries, the Soviet Union, the United States, and China defeat the Axis Powers of Germany, Italy, and Japan.
1949	Western European nations form the North Atlantic Treaty Organization (NATO) with the United States and Canada; Germany is divided into East and West.
1957	The European Economic Community (EEC) is founded.
1961–89	The Berlin Wall divides the city.
1990	Germany is reunified after the fall of the Berlin Wall.
1991	The Soviet Union breaks up into separate republics; three Yugoslav republics declare independence.
1993	The EEC becomes the European Union (EU).
2002	The **euro** replaces the currencies of 12 EU nations.
2003	The United Kingdom, Italy, Poland, and many other European nations join a **coalition** of US-led forces in the Iraq War.
2006	Serbia and Montenegro (the last of the former Yugoslav republics) become independent states.

Glossary

asylum seeker   person looking for political refuge and protection from a country

basin   area of land drained by a river or group of rivers

biodiversity   variety of plant and animal life in the world or in a particular habitat or region

biomass   all plant and animal matter, especially when used as a fuel

capitalist   referring to capitalism, a system based on the private ownership of property and wealth with free, competitive markets

climate   general weather conditions in an area over a long period of time

coalition temporary union between political parties

Cold War   state of political hostility between the Soviet bloc and the western countries, 1946–91

communist   referring to communism, a system based on the communal ownership of property and wealth with regulated markets

constituency   one of the areas into which a country is divided for a general election

continent   one of the Earth's seven huge land masses. Europe is a continent.

culinary   to do with cooking

delta   fan-shaped area at the mouth of some rivers, where the main flow splits into smaller channels

dependency   territory controlled by another country

economic migrant   person who migrates to another country to look for work and a better standard of living

environmentalist   person who is concerned about and acts to protect the natural environment

Eurasia   the total continental landmass of Europe and Asia

euro   currency common to many European countries

fjord   long, narrow, deep inlet of the sea

fossil fuel   fuel (such as coal, oil, and natural gas) that comes from the fossilized remains of prehistoric plants and animals

geyser   hot spring where boiling water and steam regularly shoot up high in the air

glacier	very slow-moving mass or river of ice, formed by compacted snow on high ground
global warming	heating up of the Earth's surface, especially caused by pollution from burning **fossil fuels**
greenhouse effect	the warming of the Earth's surface by the natural effect of a blanket of certain gases in the atmosphere. The effect is increased by gases such as carbon dioxide emitted by human activity, especially from burning fossil fuels.
gross domestic product (GDP)	total value of all a country's goods and services, not including any extra income from investment in other countries
hydroelectric power	electricity produced by moving water, especially from a dam across a river
immigration	people entering a country to settle there permanently
Industrial Revolution	rapid development of machinery, factories and industry that began in Britain in the late 18th century
Iron Curtain	imagined barrier between the Soviet bloc and the West during the Cold War
nationalism	extreme devotion to a nation that often includes feelings of being superior to other nations
parliament	a country's highest law-making body
peninsula	piece of land that juts out into the sea
plateau	flat area of high land
population density	number of people who live in a standard area (such as a square kilometre or mile)
proportional representation	electoral system in which a party gains seats in proportion to the number of votes it receives overall
Reformation	16th-century religious movement that set out to reform the practices of the Roman Catholic Church, and established Protestantism
republic	state in which power is held by the people and their elected representatives, with a president rather than a monarch
social welfare	social services provided by a state to look after its people, especially the most needy
strait	narrow passage of water connecting two seas or oceans
tributary	small branch of a larger river
wetland	land (such as marshes or swamps) that is saturated or covered with water for most of the time

Find out more

Further reading

People on the Move: Refugees and Asylum Seekers, Dave Dalton
  (Heinemann, 2005)
Continents of the World: Europe, David Flint (Wayland, 2005)
A Citizen's Guide to the European Union, Douglas Willoughby
  (Heinemann, 2006)

Websites

www.europa.eu/index_en.htm
Europa is the portal site of the European Union, providing up-to-date
coverage of EU affairs and information on European integration. You can also
access the websites of each of the EU institutions.

www.unece.org
This is the database of the United Nations Economic Commission for Europe,
very useful for up-to-date statistics.

www.friendsofeurope.org
Friends of Europe is an independent think-tank for lively EU debate.

news.bbc.co.uk/1/hi/in_depth/europe/2003/inside_europe/default.stm
Inside Europe is the BBC's guide to the changing face of the EU, and includes
information on the European Parliament.

www.eurunion.org/infores/teaching/Young/fun.htm
The website of the Delegation of the European Commission to the United
States has fun activities and shows how Americans view Europe.

www.lonelyplanet.com/worldguide/destinations/europe
This travel guide to individual European countries has 'fast facts', featured
attractions, and tourist information.

Activities

Here are some topics to research if you want to find out more about Europe:

Expanding the European Union

How many more countries should the European Union allow to join? What are the current rules for membership? Why shouldn't all countries be allowed in? Many websites deal with this issue; you could start by visiting: *http://en.wikipedia.org/wiki/Enlargement_of_the_European_Union*.

Islam in Europe

How do European Muslims and other religious or ethnic minorities fit in with their community, and how are they seen by others? You could start your research by visiting the BBC's guide to Muslims in Europe at: *http://news.bbc.co.uk/1/hi/in_depth/europe/2005/muslims_in_europe/default.stm*. The site includes a map of Muslim populations in European countries, and lots of discussion points.

Energy and conservation

Are European countries (and the European Union) doing enough to further renewable sources of energy? Should they consider nuclear energy? Are Europeans recycling enough of their waste? To help the debate, the Brussels-based Greenpeace European Unit has information at: *www.greenpeace.eu/issues/news.html*

Index